EDUCATION MANAGEMENT
in our *Society*

THE ROAD
TO SUCCESS

Dr. Iwasan D. Kejawa, Ed. D

5830 E 2nd St, Ste 7000 #9983
Casper, WY 82609
USA

TABLE OF CONTENTS

ACKNOWLEDGEMENT

Thanks to everyone that contributed to the publication of this book, directly and indirectly. Special thanks to my family.

"SO SHALL IT BE, DO THE BEST OUT THE BESTS AND
LEAVE THE REMAINS FOR EXPLORATION."

Dr. Iwasan D. Kejawa (2004).

CHAPTER I

Introduction

In the world of today, education is through motivation and satisfying the needs of learners. It is belief that the mind works wonders, and it can be substantiated with the fact that everyone can learn from each other in order to achieve the ultimate goal of each individual. Education is a conglomerate belief of individual mind. It is a security of physical, psychological, and social well beings of individual.

The technological world plays a role in education or the economy. We can infer that education is based on strategic planning. In the early stage of education for instance, we should know through history that ideas and inventions can be obtained through exploration and individual abomination. Education is the foundation of continuity, sustainability, and transformation. The group of individual learners can be the sole of success of education.

Learners can achieve their needs through critical innovation of the mind regardless of their role in society. Everyone is a learner since the educators mostly do not have control over what is to be learned in our classrooms. Society and individuals determine what they want to learn. The circumstances surrounding education and its mode of delivery may be due to affordability and security. These in turn affect the volatility and the flexibility as learner.

To eliminate doubts and worry, learners' needs must be justified by the prosperity of the societal factors. The incumbents as learners must have the resources of attaining their goals. Since learners have various goals and needs, society or organization must always embed or include scenarios and standard of accomplishments with their expectations.

The modalities of learning comprised all entities of understanding processes of humans. The dexterity of the mind can be explained through all means of communication. Both internal and external modes of communication can be justified by the learners.

The learning processes not only consist of spiritual processes, but all physical environmental, social, and technological means. The learning modes changed as one progresses through the channel of dwelling of living. Society must realize that learning yield success only when it is applied substantially through the minds of the educators and the learners. One learned most under the assumptions that he or she already possesses all the preliminary process of life within the society. As mentioned in one of the seminar sessions in the United States of America, we as humans tend to follow with able to do attitude. Acquiring self-knowledge always demands self-reflection. There is absolutely no way we can get to know ourselves if we don't take some quiet time to meditate or reflect. Contemplation is another one of the ways one tends to learn. One must be willing to open to ideas and try untested approaches and accept the risk of learning. When people are at their personal best, their projects involve creative thinking and beyond-the-boundaries thinking because of the atmospheric conditions according to them during the process of learning.

Even though some learners have gone through a process at an early stage, they must realize that nothing is done perfectly the very first time, not in schools, not in sports, not in games and certainly not in communities. We must also understand that as one evolves through changes, one tends to search for learning opportunities. Opportunities that will meet the current changes and the foresee changes. The future changes may depend on the learning materials of the present.

One's change may involve physical, psychological, and social changes as opposed to environmental changes in our society and schools. Education rests in the hands of the beholder. Educators and learners must come to agreement that we are all life-long-learners. As life-long-learners we tend to learn as we progress through life based on the needs and the consequences derived from the past. We all make mistakes and we all must learn from our mistakes which are forms of educational processes.

Again, it is my belief that mind works wonders through motivations. Learners need motivation because there is a need to motivate them to learn and this is achievable through transformation and sustainability. The longevity of humans is based on the homogeity of physical and social resources available to them. Human's adaptation is the objectivity of their consciousness. We should be aware that contemptuous circumstances can be resolved through education.

STRATEGIC EDUCATION SUPPORT

It should not be skipped from our mind that outdated traditional education, distance education, information technological infrastructures, partnerships and financial resources are common problematic issues facing many of the institutions in our world today. With this into consideration, these issues are vital to stabilize the political and economical embroidery of an institution or organization and its psychological and sociological awareness.

For education establishments to undergo a redesign phase, the modalities of both the political and economical dwellings of the establishment should thoroughly be examined and aligned. It must further be stressed that strategic change is characterized by the initiation efforts and the broad use of analytics.

Building team infrastructures will be a mandatory solution to the problematic issues facing institutions in our society today. The team infrastructure will have to include external education institutional partnership. New relationships are crucial, but only if they work at the positive task of establishing greater careers or programs coherence and the addition of both political, sociological, and economical resources. Using teams during a change effort to alleviate problems is not a new concept. It has been one of the rudiments of solving problems and making a change in history, not only in our time.

However, using teams and partnership relationships effectively in education can mean the difference between successful change and failure. As it is often said, 'With many hands, a mountain can be moved; this is to say that if we all pull together, success and power can be realized or accomplished overwhelmingly.

To involve the maximum number of incumbents in educating the populace during a process of change, improvement teams must be set up at all levels of institutions, from students and top management through frontline employees. Student organizations and government should always be included in the development and decision making at all levels. This is a way to realize the characteristics of participative democratic management in the education process.

Teamwork is one of the ingredients of attaining success and power which are the main results of what education establishments are seeking. Success in terms of monetary value is attached to private whereas public education is in terms of dignitary and ethical values. Successes of establishments must dwell on the dignitary and ethical values of the institutions even though there is instability of political and economical stance within. The economic and political instability could be overturned by consensus. These consensuses will have to do with increased input and participation; increased in both internal and external partnership relationships and increased in team efforts.

Environmental research in education will surely enable our world to predict and to achieve its optimum goals and visions of ours. Environmental research in education is in form of knowledge building which the "The capability of establishments to created new knowledge, disseminate it throughout the organization, and embody it in services and systems. Actually, services are all the efforts that are rendered that are to make institutions, the community and the inhabitants prosper. Research is a way to accumulate data, acquire knowledge, emulate, and predict solutions to certain predicament. In our case, the predicament is the economic, academics and political education situations that requires strengthening. There is an explicit and intimate link between knowledge building and internal commitment on the way to making good things happen in education. For institution establishments to succeed there must be routine environmental research in form of knowledge building. The basis of environmental scanning and knowledge building is to be performed by establishments should be coherence making, and rely on the internal and external economic, social, ethical, philosophical, and political entities or information within the establishments.

SUCCESSFUL EDUCATION EMPOWERMENT

Educating the mind is prolific and all of us as learners, both young and old, should engage in the learning process. All learners must learn the rhetoric of education as a process whereby we all learn together, including the educators.

Community, identity, stability are the main characteristics of the methodology of education in the society. As it may often conveyed in parabolic ways, stability is required of any individual if he or she is to succeed in the society. And for an individual to portray a positive identity within society educational stability will have to play a vital process in acquiring knowledge. As I always say, Knowledge comes from learning and experience while learning, and experience are respectively derived from trying and doing. Without stability and knowledge, it may be impossible to acquire success. Individuals may quest for knowledge, stability and success at an early stage of their educational career, but these entities may later be suppressed at a later stage of their life as they perceive there is no justification for learning and experience.

The possibility of attaining all the individual goals may rest solely on the individual and the society at large.

The learning process depends on the motivational level of the individual which may encompass the ingredients of success. The Ingredients of success in society may determine notions of knowledge and experience.

Education as an art to prowess is the basis of integrity in society as whole. The power of success is achievable through knowledge. The initial educational attributes of an individual suffice as learning takes place. Knowledge that is based on experience at an initial stage may result in learning activity of the present and the future.

Learning enterprise is a mode of which individual survived in the society. Accumulation of wealth may have to depend on learning, experiences, and knowledge in the society; learning, experiences, and success inevitably justaposed the amenities of wealth. The essence of educational training is the preparedness of the individual to stability and success. This may be addressed to the problematic situations of individuals in the society.

The circumstances surrounding propagation of learning are not solely materialism, but on the gratitude of knowledge. The standard which knowledge and materialism is attained are the repertoire of educational establishments. In rationalizing the commonwealth of training individual, society may have to institute transformation and sustainability in the evolution of education. The extenuation of objectives may depend on current and past activities. The educational solitudes may result in self actualization of goals and thereby create self awareness.

The technicality of learning should be justified by the scope of activities in our world Education of the literates may be different from that of illiterates in the society. Literacy does not mean everything is known, there are lessons learned from everyday activities in the society. Illiteracy of the mind is tolerable in certain aspects of learning.

The integration of learning may depend on the theme that individual need to know the anthology of surviving. Stability projects the purpose of learning current ideas in our world. The determination of success rests on stability and knowledge.

Education of the mind is cogenial to the cognitive approach of learning environment. We should believe that constant attention to the mind may gear up the learning process.

Educating the mind is a process whereby all activities are geared on the purpose of achieving positive results. All learners may have to yield to proliferation of the audacity to learn current ideas to attain success in society.

Knowledge and success are products of learning. This means that education results in knowledge and success is to attain one's goal or mission. The purpose of learning is to know what is not known and to improve what is already known. When one achieves any of these, success comes into play. Therefore, the society dwells on education because "The rudiments of living are the necessities of living on earth." One may reiterate that knowledge is power as people often says it because one's you acquire knowledge, no one could take it away from you, this means the knowledge never "dies" no matter how people try. This is to say that "One can extend life because infinity is the way of life."

EXPECTANCY OF SUCCESS

We expect success from whatever we do or engage in. It is possible for us to internally like something and feel positive toward an educator. It is also possible to have incredibly good academic concept and still not expected to succeed. Some persons might simply decide that there is not enough time to explore the avenues of success. For some people, especially the adults in the society, time is a critical issue because of their many other roles and responsibilities.

The decision to invest time in learning activities should be important as the decision to invest in efforts. Sometimes we do not understand the necessity to do well in our involvements and this confusion leads to discouragement in our activities.

Sometimes materials are so new and different to us that many of us have difficulty seeing ourselves as potential performers in necessary learning tasks. But it may be justified if we all include traditional materials of education.

There are so many different means why we might not expect to succeed; and when we do not have expectations, we can probably consider it in our best interest to be enthusiastic. If we do, we expect greater pain and disappointment if we fail. For people not to try something they do believe they can do is usually not highly intelligent, often a waste of time and discouraging.

When the expectancy for success is not certain, we tend to protect our well-being by remaining withdrawn or negative. Educators often view this as apathy or resistance, but for us it is protection and even more to do with realistic doubt than passion. In these instances, our demonstration that learning a task is strongly a position to achieve success is significantly positive influence on our attitudes. Cheerful outlook toward learning is a significant way by which success can be attained in all involvements or endeavors. A negative attitude toward education or learning creates a barrier between the knowledge to be obtained to achieve success.

CHAPTER II

Building Team Approach In Education

One of the approaches to achieving success in education is building teams and relationships with people. The use of teams during a change effort to alleviate problems has been in existence for years; it is not a new concept. However, using it effectively, team and relationship as change efforts can mean the difference between successful change and failure. To further explain, involving the greatest number of people during a change process, improvement teams should be set up at all levels of an organization, from top management through frontline employees. As I always say, 'With many hands, a mountain can be moved;' this is to say that a mission can be achieved if we all work as a team. To prosper we must involve the maximum number of people both externally and internally to realize the characteristics of participative democratic management. One cannot attain success alone. As the saying goes, "It takes two to build the world around us. The problem of lack of relationships with others could be solved by utilizing the expertise of two or more individuals. We should encourage ourselves to always adhere to the philosophy of teamwork in order to be successful.

Teams should be well organized and well coordinated. By building teams and relationships, one will be able to access the knowledge of others thus creating opportunities for increasing relationships with the outside world.

The team must be able to share knowledge about others known to them. Information as to who knows what or who of personal connections to others within could be discussed and information must be disseminated to the public so that relationships can be established. To elaborate further, from an enabling perspective, Knowledge transferred from others should be thought of as a source of inspiration and insights locally and not a direct order that must be followed. Information from the teams becomes knowledge only when it takes on a "social life."

Knowledge lies in its databases than in its people. People can spread knowledge accordingly. To build a team is to build knowledge because according to experts "Knowledge is people." It is important that we name knowledge as a core value and establish mechanisms and procedures that embody the value in action.

ORGANIZED EDUCATION RESEARCH

Increase in research all aspects of life will surely enable us to predict and to achieve our goals and visions of obtaining knowledge, establishing and increasing relationships with others; Research is in form of knowledge building that is a capability of people as a whole to create new knowledge, and disseminate it throughout the world, and embody it. Research is a way to accumulate data, acquire knowledge, emulate, and predict solutions to certain predicament. There is always an explicit and intimate link between knowledge building and internal commitment on the way to making good things happen or to achieving success. What experts are trying to make us understand is that for one to succeed there must be a routine form of knowledge building or research. The basis of research performed should be coherence making and rely on the internal and external economical and social information of the society. There will have to be an increase in organized research or knowledge building for us to alleviate the issue of lack of relationship with others. With an increase in research, one is be able to acquire abundant information and knowledge about the outside world thereby increasing the opportunity to establish relationships with suitable and compatible ones, with ultimate benefits to one.

EDUCATION AS WILL OF POWER

The concept 'will of power' strictly extends beyond leadership considerations and is associated with the philosopher Friederick Netzche. Governance and Management is an incarnation for the bewitchments of the lead. It is assumable that will of power is ubiquitous, but free will is a rarity. It follows that education governance and management is a form of life in which 'will of power' enter complex domain of conflict, reconciliation, and resolution. It is obligatory for education governance and management to find a way to settle the bewitchments of the lead.

In others word, education governance and management are the creation, organizing, managing, monitoring, and resolving values and conflicts in education – where values could be defined as concepts of desirable motivating force. To be without a mission or will would be to be without power. Will to power creates an enormous oblivious means of achieving ends. Will of power values the strategic means of traditional practice of education governance and management. In an establishment the will to achieve success rests solely on education governance and management with strong support from clients, employees and some external congruent or other people outside the establishments. These segments are the core of education governance and management. What these groups think or say determines the success of the establishments and of the people. The proprietors of society must have stability and conscience to enforce and obey rules and regulations to the escalations of success. There must be understanding of predicaments which may prevent one from achieving success in the society. These predicaments must be elaborated and justified or resolved in manners that would be of great benefit to society at large in order to achieve success in education and leading the way. The incumbents of people involved in decision making must be groomed or trained in all aspects of humanity to understand the predicaments of achieving success.

The ability to succeed in achieving the mission of an establishment depends on the values conveyed by its people and external communities. These values must be executed through participation in educating the mind; and this may be directly or indirectly. The values should be perceived by society and then conveyed to people for implementation. Education values of an institution are inter-connected with its external congruent and perceived as an integrated success of people. This is based on the facts that people tried to attain a consensus between its congruent. This consensus is indeed a will of power in education. The qualities and values of education are rational perception, ethical values, desirability, and philosophical entities.

The rationality of education hinders the achievements of success if the individual rationality of the people with which it should be exposed and compensated for their efforts. The people of society should ameliorate the bewitchments of education to obtain success.

Amelioration of activities of the management and governance in education will allow their internal and external congruencies to achieve success.

Philosophical entities or views are the promptness of success. When one exposes, airs or tenders its views in a philosophical way, then we may realize the purpose of knowledge. The quest or longing for knowledge may stimulate internal and external congruencies of every society. The reasoning of the society determines its existence. When we have positive rationality, then success would be encountered in our doings or performances. What we do with our life may be intercepted by people in society since one has no control over its involvements in the society. Society may be said to be at large.

CHAPTER III

Monachy Of Illusion In Education

Everyone in society has dreams. For one's to attain his or her dreams, one may have disillusions and illusions sometimes, that is, one may be "doubtful." Educating the mind will yield to realization of one's dreams. As it is often said by most people in society, if one puts his/her mind to achieve something, one will actually come through or achieve it. The training of the mind is a process of learning in society of ours. One must realize that the process of life is like that of a fish in the ocean, a bird in the air, animals on land, fish in the and species underground; life takes someone anywhere or everywhere. Education is an identity; what you learned sticks with you for the rest of your lifetime. It is an embroidery of life achievements. What is learned is learned and the aftermath is the rejuvenation of what is known or learned.

The issues of learning relay the economic features as well as the functionality of an individual. The aspects of political and corporate dependency should be made available in order to succeed and achieve the optimal solutions in an economy or in life. The externality of entities surrounding motivational approach is in accordance with the perception of individual as he or she is relating to the negative or positive manner of the entire populace. Some of these entities can be classified as socio-economic, ethical, political, and technological entities that keep emerging as educational trends in the society.

The establishment of ethical prowess lacks certain circumstantial environmental evidence of progressive socio-economic and technological functions. The relationships between the external factors are well documented but not adequately executed. There seems to be room for improvisations of issues concerning ethical, economical, sociological, political, philosophical and technological functions in some educational institutions and organizations. In education and generally in life all issues need to be thoroughly addressed in order to adhere to human endeavors. As it was stressed by theologians, "All things were created, and humans were created to perform improvement of the processes".

Learning as it relates to affirmative action is not adequately encouraged in all our institutions of learning. In all establishments education and economic prowess play a vital role in sustaining the integrity of individuals. Scanning of the environment is a way to perform an improvement, to better attain an overall picture of a situation, or an issue. The diversity of students as well as faculty, teachers and staff should be prioritized as it is in many establishments in society. According to various texts on cultures, diversity plays a major role. A mountain cannot be moved alone, but with many hands; that is, the impossible can be made possible with many people at work. Teamwork is an important aspect of achieving a goal.

Not breaking through the barrier of cultural differences is detrimental and deterrent to the educational awareness of many individuals. Again, there is emancipation of individualism in the global society.

The education of individuals must be elaborated eloquently and freely to meet the needs of society. The political aspect of education is ultimately demanding the economic freedom of individual and educators. The socio-economic factors as to its relationships to external environment are diminishing. The positive outcomes of the economic issues may lead to the production of high or qualified professionals. As it was mentioned in my previous writing there are confrontational issues that affect education because of environmental external conflicts. Some educational institutions and corporate institutions are lacking the substance or knowledge of achieving and producing well balanced professionals. And this is the basis of tumultuous economy.

In order to be successful we must have knowledge, positive attitudes and the understandings of the environment in which we exist. The illusions of not knowing the ingredients of success prevent individuals from attaining their goal of succeeding in society. These detriments are the justifications of failing in our endeavors. What we are involved in would pave ways to successful outcomes of economy if we all try to think intuitively in all of our involvements.

One may say that achieving success in all our engagements or involvements in life may be illusive to the perceptions of individuals involved in making decisions about our lives. The monarch of determining what is right for an individual is the intuition of the society we live in. Society is what portrays individualism. This is to say that society makes us what we are. There are set of rules, therefore, one has little or less control over his or her actions.

INDIVIDUAL BEHAVIORS

The behaviors of individuals within political establishments and educational institutions are intermittent. The behavior of individuals is dependent on one another, and is what actually determine the means of success. If we are to create a solid foundation for the betterment of society, then individual behaviors with that of political establishments and education establishments should be prone to obstacles. The behaviors of individuals should be one that can be of benefits to all in the society. As often say to people, "Life is like that of a fish in the ocean and a bird in the air, life takes you everywhere or anywhere."

If an individual is to create a rapport between each other, then everyone in the society will find it not antagonizing to belong to any of the establishments in the society. All of us in the political and educational environment should be prepared to assume an equal role in the management of society at large. As an old saying, "What comes around goes around" and "What goes around comes around." Everyone may find themselves in any atmosphere or situation.

If we are to function, then everyone in the society would be able to live their lives as they please without antagonizing each other. The behaviors of all us should be partisan and democratic. Not only would it be of benefits to us all now if we maintain good relationship, also if we do not create a rapport between each other, then some of the inhabitants in the society would exempt themselves from belonging to any establishments or organizations. We would create a chaotic society which would create bad atmospheres or situations for the present and future generations.

Individual behaviors must always have consequences, and if they have success we should reflect on the reason for their success. Cognitive psychology is the attrition theory of humans to the response of physical being and soul searching.

IMPROVEMENTS OF LEARNING

There are so many ways in which to improve education in the society. The most innovative ways are through technology and artificial intelligence. The traditional scientific ways are opaque but may sometimes rely on innovative artificial intelligence and technology. The modernization of society places traditional scientific methodologies in the dark perspectives.

There has been connotation of improvements of education of the people in the society. The improvements of learning comprised the etiology of understanding the predicaments of living in society. Natural resources are being use in all means by recollection and projection of innovations. Human behaviors and functions are conglomerations of successes and failures. That is human behaviors depend on humans' successes and failures. Immoralities result in failure and moralities result in success, so do abnormalities and formalities.

It should not skip our mind that outdated traditional way of education, information technological infrastructure, partnerships and financial resources are common problematic issues facing certain segments of the society. These considerations are important to stabilize success.

For education in a society to undergo a redesign phase, the modalities of both the political and economic dwellings of all establishments should thoroughly be examined and aligned. Furthermore, strategic change must be characterized by the initiation efforts and the broad use of analytics.

As it was mentioned earlier, building team infrastructure will be a mandatory solution to some of the problematic issues facing the society today. The team infrastructure will have to include external education institutional partnership. New relationships are crucial, but only if they work at the positive task of establishing greater careers or programs coherence and the addition of both political, sociological, and economical resources.

Using teams during a change effort to alleviate problems is not a new concept.

It has been one the rudiments of solving problems and making a change in the history of education, not only in our time. However, using teams and partnership relationships effectively can mean the difference between successful change and failure. As I say often, 'With many hands, a mountain can be moved'; this is to say that if we are altogether, working towards a common goal then success and power can be realized or accomplished overwhelmingly.

To involve the maximum number of incumbents during a change process, improvement teams must be set up at all levels of the echelon, from professionals to top educators through frontline learners. Society should always be included in the development and decision making at all institutions of learning, organizations and the government. This is a way to realize the characteristics of participative democratic process.

Learning is one of the ingredients of attaining success and power which are the main results of what establishments are seeking. Success in terms of monetary value is attached to private and public establishments in terms of dignitary and ethical values. The success of education has to do with the dwell of dignitary and ethical values of life even though there is lack of stability of political and economical stance within the society. The economic and political instability can be overturned by consensus. Some of these consensuses are realized with increase in educational awareness of the society and increase in both internal and external partnerships and relationships, and increase in team efforts.

Research surely does enable institutions to predict and to achieve its optimum goals and visions. Research is a knowledge building which allows the capability of institutions to create new knowledge, disseminate it throughout the appropriate body and encompass it in services and systems. The services are all the efforts that are rendered and being made to people in society. Research has been a way to accumulate data, acquire knowledge, emulate, and predict solutions to certain predicament. In many cases, the problems are economical, academic, and political situations that require strengthening. There is an explicit and intimate link between knowledge building and internal commitment on the way to making good things happen. For an individual to succeed there is routinely study in the form of knowledge building and educational reinforcement. The basis of study and knowledge building are forms of research. People must be cohenrent in making decisions. One must rely on the internal and external economical, social, ethical, philosophical, psychological, and political entities of making decisions.

We must adhere to the improvements of the previous and the modern, as well as gear towards new developments in our society. Education serves as a purpose for improvement of knowledge and the physical perspectives of the well being. The institutions of higher learning undergo changes in the light of technological or scientific innovations and the call for in-depth knowledge of the circumstances. Thus, education is a continuous and infinitely eloquent subject in our institution and in our society as a whole.

CHAPTER IV

Positive Leadership In Education

Education often serves as a leadership cover against improprieties of leading the way to chaotic situations. Many people in society believed that leadership skills are innate, but this is not always the case. Leadership skills can be learned through rigorous training. As leadership skills can be learned, they can also be unlearned if they are not put to practice or not updated as one proceeds through the stages of life.

In a tumultuous economy, education is an important aspect of providing leadership to people in society. Adult education is a stage where what was learned in childhood is improved upon and where new skills are acquired or learned. If one is to lead successfully in the community, he or she will have to learn new skills and update his or her old skills every now and then.

Education must be considered as a way of living our lives in society. To live our lives and to lead ourselves and others, we need to be educated to do so. Everyone must be aware of the leadership bible, so to speak, as previously expressed at the beginning of this book. As it was iterated previously – leadership is the same in education, technology, politics, and business. Leadership always has the same principles and strategies that were discussed previously.

Everyone in society is a leader some way or the other. Although this is a controversial issue, but it can be substantiated. To lead successful, a leader must collect information from his or her followers and also from other leaders and listen to their advice. He or she will have to use his or her initiatives and judgments to make a decision or lead the way. When looking at this immensely and thoroughly, the leader is not the only one leading, he or she is leading with his people. The leaders.' followers can also be considered as leaders because they do contribute their own quotas to the leadership principles and strategies in some ways. With this, we can imply that the leaders are followers and that the followers are also leaders one way or the other.

Success could be attained with the provision of positive leadership. There should be a thorough examination of leadership principles within society. The real purpose of success is for someone to feel good about oneself. Education is the right resource to get good training in making decisions about their life and to be successful. The methods of achieving success in our communities and as individual can be enumerated as follows:

Community and individual development can serve as a format for learning. Community and individual development are closely related to action projects as formats for learning. As stressed by Malcolm Knowles in his book, an increasing number of people are coming to see total communities as their classrooms – as laboratories for learning and to see their educational objectives as being not only to help individual learn to deal more effectively with their life problems, but to help communities in its entirety to deal more effectively with their problems, and to see the process of community problem solving as a vehicle for accomplishing both educational objectives. In the words of one of the education pioneers in shaping of community and individual developments, the majority of the people in the community is primarily interested in development as means of educating the people who live there.

Another way of having successful education is the formation of clubs and organized groups. The striking thing about clubs is that almost all of them have the education of their members as a central objective. As part of a comprehensive program of education, the clubs' format for learning has several unique advantages. Because it is less formal in structure and has larger social or fellowship component than most other formats, it is the method of reaching several inhabitants who might otherwise shy away from educational experience.

The acquisition of knowledge can be achieved by success of educating the people in society. The refinement of certain skills, such as communication skills, group participation skills, leisure-activity skills, leadership abilities and human-relations skills in general can be further improved by providing opportunities for the inhabitants or citizens to practice these skills and receive supportive feedback on their performance. With the provision of orientations, conventions and leadership conferences, people in our communities would be able to learn more effectively; they would also be able to assume more responsible positions within the communities. Conferences or conventions are the backbones of informal and formal positive leadership. It will be necessary to understand the various educational purposes of getting together or a conference can serve; among the possible functions of getting together may enumerated as follows:

A) Presentation of information.
B) Inspiration.
C) Exchange of Experiences.
D) Problem Solving and.
E) Commitment to Action.

One way of promoting success among people is featuring festivals, exhibits and fairs in our society. The essential feature of this format for learning is the display of ideas and processes. It is an effective format for reaching people who don't read publications, listen to broadcasts, or attend meetings, for the purpose of giving information. The exhibit may be basically a stationary sequential display, while the fair may be a non-sequential mixture of exhibits and activities, and the festival a moving display.

ISSUES OF HIGHER EDUCATION

There are so many issues involved in education for the majority of today so-called education. These issues and strategies pertain to common strategies arising in our society. Actually, we must focus on the application of leadership skills and potential strategies to address contemporary education.

During course of study, it has been discovered that emphasis in developing an increased awareness and understanding of the nature of the issues are profound to education in our society today. In order to attain success in all our endeavors we must explored the leadership strategies that can be implemented to address the issues within organizational context. We must identify and analyze issues affecting education that require leadership responses. We must be aware of how to conduct research and resource analysis. We must be able to recognize the usefulness of research in planning and implementing change strategies. We must be aware of the dynamics of planned change and how to apply change agent strategies to address issues. We should attain the knowledge to understand the range of leadership competencies and skills needed to meet challenges.

There are issues that prompt up every now and then in society and participating in leadership roles will eventually allow us to utilize all that has been learnt. The many issues of strategies involved in education may be used in solving some of the issues confronting our institutions and organizations.

The concepts of building teams and partnerships are of great interest. These concepts would always be used in any action plan that may be developed, and they may certainly be used in solving major issues confronting education. With implementations of action plan strategy, it may in the future strengthen the strategic management planning of updating leadership and management skills in solving vital issues confronting education.

One of the ways that were of value to education is "Environmental Scanning" or any research. It provided the foundations and basis of solving issues confronting education in our society today. For an organization to succeed in achieving its vision or mission, an environmental scanning or research must take place or be explored.

Another section of learning experience for success is communications. We must be aware that effective communications are the "nutshells" or strategies of solving issues confronting our society. A well thought communications strategy will be needed and this strategy would have to start with the process of strategy change. Messages will have to be linked to the strategic purpose of the change initiatives. Communications as stressed would have to be realistic and honest between all.

Another thing that is believed particularly useful and valuable in terms of my own experience is "Team: Building the Infrastructure for Effective Change". It made us aware that besides establishing the need to change and developing a vision of what success will look like, building team infrastructure to create change should be one of the first tasks management undertakes. It was advised that management should start identifying the team structure and members as early in the change process as possible. Teams should consist of the steering committee, the integration team and improvement team. With the improvement team, the typical team includes team leader, management, employees, ad hoc team members, and a facilitator. Members of the improvement teams should have a working knowledge of the process being changed.

To be successful in education of the mind, taking online courses is in fact like being in the classroom. Online is as effective as that of the classroom mode. Chat sessions are just like that of instructions delivered in a classroom. The notes and lecture modules posted are valuable instruments in achieving success; they were indeed similar to actual handouts in the live classroom. It is always an experience worthwhile.

FALLACY OF SUCCESS IN EDUCATION

To attain success at the optimum level, we need to pave the optimum performance. The myth of successful education is relayed in the mission and vision of every institution. Attaining success depends on the strategies laid out in the materials of goals setting (mission and vision) and achieving the results of those goals. Goals are included or embedded in the mission and vision of every institution. The education of an individual is part of his/her mission and vision statement since education is derived from learning and learning comes trying. Education is the knowledge of learning what is most important in life - this also applied to any institution of learning.

Success can only come about from knowledge and education. In order to acquire knowledge and success, education or learning must first take place. Without education of some sort, there will be no knowledge and success. As has been mentioned earlier in this book, education can takes place anywhere and in any forms. What really matters is the knowledge. Education, knowledge, and success are intersected. They both cross the same pathways.

Achieving success may be misleading at times because success is not at a constant rate. Education is necessary if we are to achieve success, and education is also not at a constant rate.

Education varies from time to time. What one learns at a certain point of life may have to be improved by learning new ideas, that is either by refreshing old skills or learning new skills. As it has been mentioned before in my books, this may be to as "Lifelong learning".

Educating beginners and the professionals is a fallacy of success because learning comes at a point in time.

Who really needs an education? This is a controversial topic. One needs to be educated as one progresses through the life stages. Education or the process of learning is both for the young and the old. Old habits may have to be unlearned to compensate for new habits.

Actually, to achieve success, only bad habits should be unlearned and the good habits improved upon by updating old skills and learning new ones.

As mentioned earlier free will of power is rarity; there is always some stigma attached to ones being successful. Sometimes we must forgo or involve ourselves negatively. Negativity sometimes results in positivism after adjustments and performances of functions or activities.

One must work, perform and endure the rigorous life. In a biblical sense, God gave us the ingredients of success. We must then find ways to use what is given to better ourselves. In other to be successful we therefore work, perform, live our lives, and endure the rigor refining what has been given to us by God. For example, in the early biblical days there were no automobiles or aircrafts, but humans used all the resources available to successfully develop the means of transportation. This is just an example.

Computer technology is also another example. Along the way, there are consequences or prices paid for being successful. Therefore, free will is rare. The will to power rests solely on the understanding of the cohorts of the society or organization. The behaviors and the engagements of the activities of the society determine its success.

ACCUMULATION OF WEALTH

The accumulation of wealth may lead to success in monetary terms, but without proper education wealth may result in failure as one trend through the stages of life. It is not only money that makes someone happy or successful. Happiness is a result of being successful and success is a result of being happy. Both success and happiness are intertwined. They both have related causes.

One may be happy and not successful, and one may be successful and not happy. The goal in life is for someone to be happy and successful monetarily and health wise. The education of the mind plays an important role in achieving happiness, success, and good health.

Once we are healthy and happy, then we are successful. We must protect ourselves from being unhappy, unsuccessful, and unhealthy by having or equipping ourselves with all the ammunition of education entities. Educational entities comprised of the economical, sociological, political, psychological, physiological, technological, and scientific embroideries of life.

The educational entity is based on what constitutes technology in the modern society. There is a correlation between what education is of the past, the present and the future. In today's world, wealth is base on knowledge, education, values and pragmatic approach.

The educational approach is what constitutes management tools. Wealth management is of great importance as well as education in globalization. The past, present, and future terms are reciprocity of the globalization.

The retention of wealth and knowledge serves the purpose of conservatism and pragmatic values and approach. Changes are preserved in our institutions. These changes are pragmatic to the management and well-being of the society and individuals. Education is a co-existence of values and desire. The philosophical entity is composed of resources and performance.

The composition of wealth is the entity of products in the global market. The consistency of educational products are based on the magnitudes of the information obtained from the past and present. Models and consistencies are aligned with extensive extenuation of objectivity of technology. With the extenuation of objectives, there are subjectivities to innovations. The past may be subjective to the development of the modern. Educational products and information are inter-changeable commodities in technological society. The aspect of globalization is empowered through local development of external entities. The adaptability of external local entity serves as philosophical globalization.

The configuration of external foreign entities, such as tools of the past era results in a commonwealth of technology. Technological and scientific posterities serve as the philosophical view of the modern. As a result of technological and scientific innovations there is a prowess in perspective and convenience. Information and educational commodities are internally and externally displayed and stored technologically or scientifically. The value of information or educational commodities are the logical dwellings of philosophical abstracts of technology and science.

Accumulation of wealth depends on innovation of both present and past era to attain, simplicity, sophistication and adaptability. This presents the future with everlasting and endurance of tools in society. Technology is adeptly the invigoration of educational expertise in our society. The combinations of know-how, when and why are attributed to the development and enhancement of situations, ideas, products and their awareness.

CHAPTER V

Education Of Professionals

The production of well-qualified professionals to meet the demand of the growing population is a vital issue in our society today. There is a short fall in meeting the production of well qualified professionals. The demand for well-qualified professionals in the society calls for more and rigorous education of every individual in the society. Due to the shortages of well qualified professionals and increased demand by the community/society, there should be an increase in the enrollments of learners at several institutions in the society. In other to satisfy the demand of the society and to meet the demand for good quality education, we need well qualified professional educators.

Professional education is an important aspect of living and achieving success in society. There is a justification for producing the best professionals, including educators, to satisfy the demand and the needs of the society. The education profession consists of both the economical, sociological, psychological, physiological, and technological functionalities to meet the increase elevation of discoveries and innovations in the professional arena. The focus is on the production of well qualified professionals and also the attraction of well-educated professionals to serve as educators. Overview of the development of professionals must be thoroughly examined and aligned with its production.

There have been so many scientific, technological, political, and socio-economic developments in recent years concerning effects of the production of well qualified educators and non-educators. According to the article in one of the professional journals titled: "Surged in the Number of Professionals;" it was stated that the recent increased in the Malpractices lead to the withdrawal of many professionals from practicing, thereby causing an increase in unemployment.

Professional Education has an impact on how successful we are. There is an impact in the increase in education of professionals today as a result of increased enrollments of learners and unemployment. There is a need for well-qualified professionals, in other to meet the demand of the population. Environmental scanning provides the basic elements surrounding producing good professionals and increase in enrollment of learners and its impact on education.

According to research performed by Time Magazine, on professions in America, the issue of producing and attracting well qualified professionals depends on having a well balanced mixed education, socio-economic and political preparedness. There is a call for professionals as the aging overall population increases and as the enrollments of learners increase. The overall population is not at a standstill, there is always an increase in the population of infants, adolescence, adults and elderly in our society. This calls for the production of well-educated professionals, including educators.

Extrapolation in education may hinder the successful production of professionals in a way if we do not take into considerations proper admission criteria into professions. There may be certain hidden qualities of students or Learners, therefore, the basis of admissions to professions should be greatly examined or carefully looked into.

There will continue to be an increase in the number of enrollments of students or learners in various professions, as long as the population increases, and as long as there is a growing demand for well qualified professionals. We should also be aware that the longevity of humans is the homogeneity of the body, and the spontaneity of the adaptability is the objectivity of the consciousness. This is to say that as we live our life, our physical performance diminishes and the way we adapt also diminished but our mentality depends on our consciousness. If the professionals are to meet the demands of the society, they must be prepared to be well rounded or mixed education or training of their mind.

If society does have well trained professionals, then the society will be well placed and this will result in good practices globally, otherwise the society will be in jeopardy or bad situation and mal practices will continue to rise. If educational institutions are able to attract well qualified learners and professionals, there will be an increase in the number of research, innovations and applications. To use the present available ammunitions of wealth, there is the need for well trained professionals; and the training of professionals and learners can be achieved by encouraging the practitioners to assume teaching professions.

If the enrollments of learners continue to increase, there will be a great need for well-trained educators in our society. Also there will be an increase in the number of well qualified graduates to satisfy the increased demand of services by the population. It should be noted that if we do not have well educated professional educators, there will be chaos in society because we will be producing incapable professionals and living chaotic lives. Because this may lead to an increase in the number of mal practices in the various professions which in turns may be chaotic. As a result of all these outcomes, there will be a stigma to professions which will in the long run jeopardize the continuation of enrollment of learners and entrance into a profession. Reduced enrollment of learners may lead to the unemployment of all professionals including educators. Also, an increase in professional practices expenses may make the practitioners to change professions. It may also be implied that without a balanced well-trained educators and learners, technology or scientific innovations of professions will be adamant; that is these innovations will be frozen or be at a standstill.

ELONGATION OF POWER

The length of power strictly extends beyond leadership considerations, and it is generally associated with education and management. Power is an incarnation of the bewitchments of the lead. It is assumable that power is ubiquitous, but mere power is a rarity. It follows that education power is a form of life in which elongation of power enters into complex domain of conflict, reconciliation, and resolution.

In others word, power is the creation, organizing, managing, monitoring, and resolving values and conflicts – where values may be defined as concepts of desirable motivating force. To be without a goal or desire would be to be without power. Elongation of power creates an enormous oblivious means of achieving a goal and desire. Elongation of power may value the strategic means of achieving success. In society, achieving success rests solely on elongation of power with strong support from the inhabitants or citizens.

The ability to succeed in achieving the mission of society depends on the values conveyed by its citizens. These values are executed through the participation of individuals directly or indirectly. Values are conceptually perceived by leaders which are then conveyed to individuals in the society for implementation. The values of society are inter-connected where values are considered to be perceived as an integrated success of people in the society. This is based on the facts that we tried to attain a consensus between members of society. This consensus is indeed the elongation of power within society. The qualities and values of power are rational perceptions, ethical values, desirability, and philosophical entities.

CHANGING ENTITIES IN EDUCATION

Even though we are satisfied with a situation, changes still need to be made to better our life. Satisfaction is a process where one is content with a situation, but a situation depends on several other situations. There at times when one is satisfied with a situation, one may still need to change that situation by changing the entities that are attached to the situation or justified with the situation.

In society, changes must be made, so as to realize the goals of existence. As it was stated in one of my books: Reaching the Heights: "Resources have been made available to human beings from the creation; it is up to us individuals to refine the resources." For instance, we have brain and mind, thus it's up to individual to stimulate or train the brain and mind, and to use them accordingly. Through education we can meet the process of changing entities in our society.

Education is the key to success; without education nothing could be realized or achieved. If we do not learn the rhetoric of taking care of ourselves, then we will not be in existence. We have to wake up and keep going if we are to achieve success in this world.

Changes of entities do not necessitate the change of entire procedures. We can make changes by updating the traditional ways of doing things, through innovations and research this may be realized by education which is a means of stimualting and training of the brain and mind to acquire knowledge. It is also possible to make an entire change of situations or traditional ways of doing things through research and technology. Thus, changing of entities or situations is vice versa. For instance, we can make an innovation to a marriage vow by asking the couples to mix water, red wine and their blood together and tell each of them to drink the mixture. This will signify that they are both joined together and this signifies they not be separated until death comes their way because it is very difficult to separate water from wine or red wine and blood by human. The couple becomes one because they both internally absolve the concussion of each other being. The only possible thing possible that can be done by humans is to immerse or put certain things or chemicals into the mixture to turn the mixture back to water or something else by purifying the individual internal body.

THE EDUCATION PROWESS

Leadership is somehow an elongated educational means of achieving prosperity and power, but it is a well to do way of attaining success. The leadership processes and strategies are usually based on the strengths that build the foundations of a group or community involved in management and governance. The governance and management of an organization or community can be straightened by thoroughly examining and improving the education of its leaders and members.

The leaders in the community can attain ultimate powers by listening to the people and adhering to the law of the community. Leaders would be able to exercise power and control if and only if the leadership principles and strategies are explored and enforced in positive ways.

Education will play a vital role in providing leadership education to people in modern society. Adults are more experienced in leading the way to success because they are more matured, and most adults are opened to new ideologies. Adults are also willing to update their old skills in a safe, secure and sound environment. Educating both young and olds to assume leadership roles in society is a means by which the society can cure its socio-economic maladies. Leadership education should be introduced to people at all levels of the departments in our institutions. Many learners and educators should be delegated to assume leadership in their specializations. As education is a conglomeration of various subjects, so is leadership. Leadership can be said to comprise the execution of strategies and decisions by a group of incumbents in an organization or community. Educational leadership is a process where a driver steers the passengers in a safe way to their desired destination or destinations. It is a way of leading the flocks to success with little or no glitches.

LEADERSHIP ETIQUETTE IN EDUCATION

The leaders in our society should imperatively be indulged in education. If leadership process is embraced by education at all levels, then we would be able to have leaders with a broad perspective view of our needs in the society, which in turns will in turns embellish performance in all their endeavors. Leadership etiquette has momentum in accomplishing the social and economic objectives of our lives. Leadership etiquette may serve as the backbones of economic and political stability. With leadership etiquette, the society will be able to function in all avenues of its economic and social needs by yielding well rounded and educated leaders; the leaders that would be able to apply knowledge and experiences. We should be aware that, with leadership, politics play a big part. Conversely, in politics, leadership etiquette will have to play a bigger part.

The behaviors of leaders with that of political establishments and educational institutions in which they belong are intermittent. Behaviors of Leaders depend on each other. If we are to create a solid foundation for the betterment of society, then leadership behaviors with that of political establishments and education establishments would be prone to obstacles. The behaviors of all leaders should be one that can be of benefit to all in the society. As often say to people, "Life is like that of a fish in the ocean and a bird in the air, life takes you everywhere or anywhere."

If all leaders are to create a rapport between each other, then everyone in society will find it not antagonizing to belong to any of the establishments in the society, and therefore attained some kind of success in their endeavors. If we do not create a rapport between each other, then some of the inhabitants in the society would exempt themselves from belonging to any establishments or organizations and thereby failing. This would create a chaotic society which would create a bad atmosphere or situations for the present and future generations.

All organizations, including political and educational organizations, should be prepared to assume an equal role in the management of the society at large. As an old saying "What comes around goes around" and "What goes around comes around." Everyone may find themselves in any atmosphere or situation.

If we are to function, then everyone in the society would be able to live their lives as they please without antagonizing each other. The behaviors of all leaders should be partisan and democratic. Not only would it be of benefits to us all but would ease and eliminate the confusions in the society.

Many leaders provide everlasting umbrella or cover to the followers or the society in its entirety. Good etiquette could be regarded to mend the gap of their leadership and the behaviors of others – others may either be followers or leaders. Leadership is to be learned to accumulate all the necessary ingredients of governing from the people, and to implement new ideas regardless of the obstacles that may be encountered during the process of leading the flocks.

Leadership etiquette should nevertheless be used to reflect and to document all the fruitful and unfruitful decisions made during the leaders' absence. We should allow the present and future generation of leaders to learn from the mistakes made by former leaders and to improve and embellish their fruitful decisions and accomplishments. New leaders arise from the old generation of leaders and its followers within the absence of a leader. A great number of people in society should be prepared to assume leadership roles during the absence of a leader. Everyone is capable of leading, thus providing opportunities to lead in our society of ours should be economical, social, political, and democratic. Conservatism does not play an enormous part in leading the people in our society.

Leaders in our society should increase their motivational self awareness. Industry, schools, and business should be filled with well-designed, efficient instructional programs that are very motivating. Part of the predicament should not be efficiency itself. Motivation takes people-to-people skills and time. Like an excellent conversation, it cannot be rushed. The best way to see motivational strategy is an investment. It pays dividends but often not immediately.

Also, what motivates people is often beyond the inherent structure of the knowledge or skill they are learning, leaders have to plan for motivation in its own right. It cannot be taken for granted. A motivational Framework for Culturally Responsive Teaching can be used as an organizational aid instructional leadership planning. It is a systematic way of applying motivational strategies throughout a learning sequence.

The perception of one's role as a leader should be viewed as generally incompatible with the roles that are authoritarian and directive but very effective with those that are collaborative, egalitarian, and consultative.

Culture, experience, and talent really count in attaining success and investing in leadership in a tumultuous society. When the majority decides whether to back an organization or community, they look for three things – the marketability of the organization, the capacity to deliver its mission or product, and the ability of the founder to sustain excellence and grow new leaders; all these commonalities are important in investing and providing leadership in a community or organization.

Leaders who can manage talent possess four traits which are enumerated as follows:

First of all, the willingness to take risks; and even some founders have with that. It is absolutely right that everyone fears failure, fears moving into new dimensions or frontiers; and that fear only gets worse in bigger organizations. But successful leaders have great confidence. They know how to operate in a discomfort zone. They are not afraid to employ people who are smarter than themselves, especially to complement an acknowledged weakness.

Secondly, leaders should be good communicators. This means that they must be able to communicate their marketability to everyone. If a leader lacks these presentation skills, then he or she should be educated accordingly.

Third, most successful leaders are decisive. They're faced with making a lot of decisions quickly, but as discussed earlier on, these leaders learn the fine distinction between decisive and authoritarian – a skill in which relative inexperience leader is most telling. Society needs set of assumptions in which to base its plan, its mission and strategy. These assumptions would give a leader, when lost in making decisions, an avenue to remember the fundamental that drive success.

Fourthly and somehow the most important one is intellectual honesty attribute. From the minute one decides to be a member of organizations, one should always air our concerns with the leaders. One should be sure to stress the weaknesses of the leaders, not to demoralize the leaders but to help them grow. Without open, ongoing exchange among members and leaders you get cheerleading and not leadership.

EMPATHY OF SOPHISTICATIONS

The empathy of sophistications in achieving success can be resolved in our life if we take time to rejuvenate our intentions. It has come to the past that the experience of difficulties may be due to misunderstanding of our world.

When one is satisfying the intricacies of experience, then success is achievable. Education of the mind is a way of satisfying the intricacies of experience. The sophistications encountered along the way of one's life may contribute to one's stability, thus making ones goal achievable. When we realize our goal, then we are said to be successful in our endeavors.

The sophistications of understanding other people's feelings or experiences are what prevent us from attaining success. In other words, we must seize to have empathy, since empathy sophisticates or jeopardizes the realization of our missions or visions in life which are to be successful in what we do. Not eliminating the difficulties of understanding one another is detrimental to achieving success and it is the determinant of the failure of successful education. Learning the rigors of life relies on the education of the mind as already specified and elaborated in various educational materials and texts.

In order to be successful learning must take place. Without learning, absolutely no one can attain success in his endeavors. We must realize that occupying our time with positive activities is forms of learning to be successful; while engaging in negative episodes will not yield success.

It should come to light that evolution is a process of learning. We must learn to make creations up to our advantage. What was created in life must be made better in order to live our life in prosperous and convenient ways.

In a biblical sense, we must find ways to better what God has given us, and in other to do this education or learning comes into the picture. Those that learn the bad ways of disrupting the works of others will not succeed in life. As I often say religiously, 'those with derogatory powers of divinity are children of God's fire and those with sacred are children of God kingdom.'

CHAPTER VI

Management Of Infrastructures

In a turbulence situation or society, the management of infrastructure must be thoroughly examined and aligned at all facets. The educational aspects must be explored, and innovations provided technologically. Institutions must be made aware of all options of innovative processes. There should be no backlash or finger-pointing if we are to succeed in governing and managing tumultuous situation.

Improvements to the ways things are done should be common grounds with decisions makers. It is when things are improving that innovations take place. New ideas give birth to technologically innovative infrastructure. During the cause of improving a product, new ideas suffice as a result of information and product management.

Industries should engage in training and education of the people at all levels of the corporate echelon. In a tumultuous education environment or economy, it is the best practice to have well trained or educated personnel to propel the vitality of our resources. Resources from all sorts of avenues should be realigned with proper education to achieve success. Education serves as a means of achieving success in all our endeavors. One should be aware that success is not only on monetary or wealth terms. It is that satisfaction of inner soul or inner feeling so to speak. It is the realization of one's goal or vision. One can be successful without money or wealth if one realizes what he or she wants to achieve in life. Each of our resources is made possible through educating the mind.

The human resource efforts of all our educational institutions or industries should be maximized to attain optimum performance; and the costs of production or yielding outputs should be minimized to embellish profits if we are to succeed in turbulent situation or environment. We should be aware that costs of yielding outputs depend on human resource efforts and qualities of education. To minimize costs, we should find ways to fund educational establishments and our corporate industries and reduced tuitions and eliminate loans. One suggestive way or method is to increase taxes of households with two more children and those with higher education degrees or well to do individuals, the so-called millionaires and billionaires.

This may indirectly also solve other economic and social problems. One of the problems it may solve is overpopulation because people may feel reluctant to have many children. And this may in the long run solve the economic and social issues such as inflation, unemployment, and congestion of the populace on our hands today and the foresee future.

The management of infrastructure of educational facilities also plays an important role in achieving overall success in a tumultuous education environment. We must make sure that all amenities are put into place for educating our citizens. Education depends on the economic and political situations of the society. Without economic and political stability of a community, educating the inhabitants will be strenuous and nearly impossible. Education, economic and political stabilities of a community or country are intertwined.

In a tumultuous education environment, economic and political turbulence should always be resolved so that success can be achieved in educational areas. An improved economy and stable politics will eventually lead to perfect education of the inhabitants, and a perfect education will also improve the economic and political situations in the long run.

POSITIVE SELF-CONCEPT

To achieve success in a tumultuous education environment, one must develop a positive self-concept toward learning. It is believed that the greatest evil that befall someone is that he or she should come to think ill of himself or herself. Some learners may not have negative attitude toward educators, but they may have negative attitude toward themselves. Learners may believe that their capabilities to perform a task and succeed at it are inadequate or weak. Someone of such negative beliefs is often refers to have a "poor self-concept". The person's motivation to learn is often reduced or diminished.

It is common among adults, self-concept may be situation-specific. A person might feel quite physically adept but very incompetent in academic situations. This kind of difficulty also exists within the academic self-concept. A learner may feel quite superior in English and very inferior in Mathematics. Adults constantly modify their self-concepts in specific areas of learning, which means that during instructional or training session we have a great chance to positively affect a person's self-estimation.

Nevertheless, we must have cautions, adults especially have a firmer and more fully developed self-concept than do children. It is not common for us as adults to harbor doubts about our personal learning ability. We often underestimated and underused our capabilities to no avail. Sometimes our family members may reinforce our self-doubts by questioning our abilities or need for certain learning or education. Many learners are prone to this source of anxiety later in old age periods and adulthood.

Regardless of the state of one's self-concept, especially that of adult's, on entering learning situation, we can provide the experiences from which each one can derive self-confidence as a learner or student. The fundamental for acquiring a positive self-concept for learning in any area is realistically seeing one-self as a successful learner from one's own perspective.

People, especially adults are inclined toward autonomy in many aspects of their daily lives; the following methods to escalate their sense of personal causation while learning should effectively complement this tendency. People as leaner plan and set goals for learning. Planning validates the individual as the originator and guide of the process. To the extent appropriate, the learners makes choices about what, how, with whom, where, and when to learn something. Choosing is the essence of responsibility. It permits the learner to feel ownership of the learning experience. Learners can choose topics, assignments, with whom to learn, when to be evaluated, how to be evaluated and so forth. People as learners may also use self-assessment procedures. When learners appraise mistakes and successes while learning, they experience a concrete sense of participation in the learning act. Sometimes learners can get the feelings that mistakes are created by the educator more than committed by the learner. Self-assessment procedures can prevent this misconception because all is in the hands of the learner. Also, self-assessment procedures give the learner a sense of control from the beginning to the end of the learning experience. When a person can determine for himself or herself whether she is really learning something, then he or she will feel more responsible for that learning.

Educators should help the learners to identify strengths while the learners learn. For instance, the educator may say, "You have several assignments to choose from, but it seems to me that you have a real talent for explaining things well and could probably give a very interesting oral presentation. What do you think?" A learner who knows and takes advantage of personal assets while learning will feel a real sense of power and confidence.

People as learners logs personal progress while or during learning process. This allows them as learners, to feel personal growth concretely as it takes place. Successful would-be learners participate in analyzing potential blocks to progress in learning. For example, the educator may question: "What do you think the difficulty may be?" or, "In your estimation, where do you think the confusion begins?" By getting involved in solving problem, the learners feel more committed to its resolution and are more aware of their roles in the learning process. This is a bonus for educators because some people especially adult learners frequently know better where problem in learning are occurring.

When it is advisable, learners must make a commitment to learning tasks. Actually this accentuates the learners' personal choice. It may eliminate denial or withdrawal of personal responsibility for learning. When one asks a learner, "Are you sure you're going to do that you're going to try?" and one receives a sincere affirmative answer, then one knows he or she is helping invigorate the learner's sense of self-determination. This kind of technique must be used sparingly and with care forethought. It seems if it lacks integrity, it may become a mere manipulation and an insult to the learner. It is advised that one should be cautious.

The purpose of these positive self-concept methods is to show that most of the responsibility for learning is under the control of the learners. For someone, especially adults to feel "I can do it" when it comes to future learning, he or she must have felt "I did it" during previous experiences in learning.

MOTIVATIONAL STRATEGIES

In tumultuous education environment, learners must be highly motivated. There are various strategies in motivating people to learn successfully. It is common to motivate people to learn by physically rewarding them with materials or money, but this is not the best solution. There are various other ways to motivate people to achieve success. These strategies of motivating people to succeed can be enumerated as follows: People should be encouraged to learn the best way they can. This type of strategy can be used with a group or an individual.

Encouragement is any behavior on our part by which we show people that we respect them as individuals; that we trust and believe in their learning efforts to learn; and that the learner can learn. People who perceive that educator's or instructor's respect is contingent only to learning performance may feel dehumanized. Such criterion for acceptance by educator or instructor denies one's other worthy qualities and makes the person into a "thing" that learns without feelings or dignity. The primary foundation for encouragement is our caring about and acceptance of the learner. Acceptance and caring create the context in which we chose the ways to show confidence and personal regards for learners' efforts and achievements. These ways include the following:

1). Giving recognition for efforts.
2). Minimizing mistakes while people are struggling.
3). Emphasizing learning from mistakes.
4). for every learning task, demonstrating a confident and realistic expectancy that learner will learn.
5). Showing faith in the people capacity to learn.
6). Working with people at the beginning of a difficult task.
7). and affirming the process of learning.

One other motivational strategy is to promote the learners' personal control of the context of learning. This is very important because learners need to be successful and feel encouraged, but for people to build confidence as learners, people usually need to realize that their own behaviors are most responsible for their learning. This is especially the case for people with individualist values; they are more compelled to feel a sense of personal causation in the process of learning-that they mainly control how, what, and what they learn regardless of the educator's perception. At first, this may seem obvious: if a person studies, pay attention, and practices, of course the person will feel responsible any successful achievements. However, when we remember that educators or instructors are the ones who usually establish requirements, issue assignments, give tests, generally set standards for achievements, often control the learning environment and sometimes pressure the learners' involvements, it is not too surprising to understand how a learner could come to believe that it is the educator who is most responsible for their achievements. Even when a person is successful, he or she may feel very dependent as a learner and consequently bound to the demands and directions of the educators for future learning. Somehow, in this way, a person feels like a zombie while learning and not develop self-confidence as a learner.

To motivate people to learn, using the strategy where learners have access to prompt feedback or response is essential. Prompt feedback during learning leads to stronger feelings of personal control and responsibility. This is absolutely one of the reasons computer-assisted instruction is fantastic for increasing motivation. The computer has the mechanical ability to give immediate feedback or response. The learners have moment-to-moment awareness of their progress in learning. This constant back-and-forth dialogue between the computer and the learners gives the learners a strong sense of control in learning process. In so many instances, the computer conveys to the learners it will not respond until the learners respond first. The learners' personal control is undeniable.

In comparison, the longer it takes for someone to know if a response has had an effect, the more difficult it can become to know whether that response at all had any effect. For example, imagine having a conversation with a person who waited at least a minute or longer to answer or respond to any of the questions you asked him or her. It is likely that you would wonder if you were heard.

It should be noted that anything educators, particularly instructors can do to ensure that best possible pace of accurate feedback or response will concretely or immensely help to emphasize learners responsibilities.

CHAPTER VII

Committed Efforts

Efforts are made to realize results or outcomes, be they negatives or positives. Committed efforts are those which are firmly implemented to realize a goal no matter what the situations or outcomes may be. This is based on the facts that in the society we have nothing to loose in managing our lives. All attempts or efforts have to do with risk management to attain our goals through committed efforts or not.

Committed efforts to obtain success in all endeavors or dwellings do not eliminate risk management but assure success because of the determination exerted to succeed relies on the risk factors of the attempts or efforts. When all attempts or efforts are considered or made, then the risk factors of making mistakes impose greater chances of succeeding. There are always obscurities or obstructions along the paths or means of our endeavors, but we must keep trying. If we fail one time or numerous times, there is certainly going to be a time that we will succeed because the world is built on failure and success.

There are no perfection in everything but compromise. Everything is built on skepticisms or per say.

It should be clear that what you realize from what you do is what matters. Realizing an outcome is the recognition of all the efforts or attempts. We must substantially and accurately acknowledge our success to the capability of all efforts and knowledge. This makes it clear that all itineraries or housekeeping should be analyzed, concluded, and implemented.

Some people may be discouraged when they realize how much extra time it takes to master the subjects that are being taught. However, people's attitudes can easily be influenced positively when the following three conditions are guarantee: 1) the qualities of instruction that will help people learn if they try to learn. 2) The concretes proof of evidence that people's efforts make a difference. 3) The continual feedback regarding the progress of learning. In addition, it helps the educators to realize that some people know for certain how much time and effort it takes to achieve success in a particular subject or involvement. When these three stated conditions are present from the very first beginning of a subject, people have a much better chance to attain success. Successes are attained at large when these conditions are explored thoroughly in context.

EDUCATION THROUGH MOTIVATION

Education is through motivation, accommodations, and satisfying the needs of learners. It is believed that an educated mind is wonderful, and this can be substantiated with the fact that everyone can learn from each other in order to achieve the ultimate goal of each individual. Education is believed to be a conglomerate of well-groomed individual minds. It is the security of physical, economical, psychological, and social well beings of individual.

The technological world also actually plays a role in the development of education. It can be said that education is based on strategic planning. In the early stage of adult education,

It has been noted through history that ideas and inventions were obtained through exploration and individual abomination. Education is the foundation of continuity, sustainability and transformations. A group of individual learners can be the sole of success of education.

Learners can achieve their needs through critical innovation of the mind regardless of their role in society. Everyone is an adult learner since the educators do not have control over what is to be learned in our classrooms. Society and individual determine what they want to learn. The circumstances surrounding education and its mode of delivery may be due to affordability and security. These in turn affect the volatility and the flexibility as learner.

To eliminate doubts and worry, learners' needs must be justified by the prosperity of societal factors. The incumbents as learners must have the resources of attaining their goals. Since adult learners have various goals and needs, society or organization must always embed or include scenario and standard of accomplishments with their expectations.

The modalities of learning comprised all entities of understanding processes of humans. The dexterity of the mind can be explained through all means of communication. Both internal and external modes of communication can be justified by the learners.

The learning processes not only consist of spiritual processes, but all physical environmental and technological means. As an adult the learning modes changed as one progresses through the channel of dwelling of living. Society must realized that learning yield success only if it is applied substantially through the minds of the educators and the learners. We learned mostly under the assumption that we possess already all the preliminary process of life within the society. As mentioned earlier on, we as humans tend to follow with a can-do attitude. Acquiring self knowledge always demands self reflection. There is absolutely no way we can get to know ourselves if we don't take some quiet time to meditate. Contemplation is another one of the ways adults tends to learn. Most adults are willing to open to ideas and will try untested approaches and accept the risk of learning. When people are at their personal best, their projects involve creative thinking and beyond-the-boundaries thinking because of the atmospheric conditions according to them during the process of learning.

Even though learners have gone through a process at an early stage, we must realize that nothing is done perfectly the very first time, not in schools, not in sports, not in games and certainly not in communities. We must also understand that as adults evolve through changes, they tend to search for learning opportunities; opportunities that will meet the current changes and the foresee changes. The future changes may depend on the learning materials of the present.

Changes may involve physical, psychological, and social changes as opposed to environmental changes in our society and schools. Education rests in the hands of the beholder. Educators and learners must come to agreement that all people are life-long learners. As life-long learners we tend to learn as we progress through life based on needs and consequences derived from the past. As mistakes are made, we all learn from our mistakes which are forms of the educational process.

It is my beliefs that minds are wonderful through encouragement. Learners need motivation because there is a need to encourage them to learn, and this can be achieved through transformations and sustainability. Actually, the longevity of learners is based on physical resources available to them. Learners' adaptation is the objectivity of their consciousness. It should be noted that contemptuous circumstances can be resolved through education.

Educating the mind is prolific and all adults, both learners and educators should engage in the learning process. Both learners and educators must learn the rhetoric of education as a process whereby we all learn together, including the educators.

Community, identity, stability are the main common characteristics of the methodology of education in the society. As it is often conveyed in parabolic ways, stability is required of any individual if he or she is to succeed in the society. And in order for an individual to portray a positive identity within the society, educational stability will have to play a vital role in acquiring knowledge. As it is often said, Knowledge comes from learning and experience while learning and experience are respectively derived from trying and doing. Without stability and knowledge, it may be impossible to acquire success. Individual may quest for knowledge, stability, and success at early stage of their educational career, but these entities may later be suppressed at a later stage of their life as they find that there is justification for learning.

The possibility of attaining all the individual goals may rest solely on the individual himself and society at large.

The learning process depends on the motivational level of the individual which may encompass the ingredients of success. The ingredients of success in society may determine the notions of knowledge and experience. Education is an art to prowess as the basis of integrity in the society. The power of success is achievable through knowledge. The initial educational attributes of an individual suffice as learning takes place. Knowledge which is based on experience at an initial stage may result in learning activity of the present and future.

Learning enterprise is a mode of which individual survived in the society. Accumulation of wealth may have to depend on the knowledge and experience in society; learning and success inevitably juxtaposed the amenities of wealth. The essence of educational training is the preparedness of the individual to stability and success. It must be addressed to the problematic situations of individuals in the society.

The circumstances surrounding propagation of learning is not solely materialism, but on the gratitude of knowledge. The standard which knowledge and materialism is attained is repertoire of educational establishments. In rationalizing the commonwealth of training individual, the Society may have to institute transformations and sustainability in the evolution of education. The extenuation of objectives may depend on current and past activities. The educational solitudes may result in self actualization of goals and thereby create self awareness.

The technicality of learning may be justified by the scope of activities in society. The education of the literates may be different from that of illiterates in the society. Literacy does not mean everything is known, there is lessons to be learned from everyday activities in society. Illiteracy of the mind is tolerable in certain aspects of learning.

The integration of learning may depend on the theme that individual needs to know the anthology of surviving. Stability projects the purpose of learning new ideas in our world. The determination of success rests on stability and knowledge.

Education of the mind is substantial to the cognitive approach of learning environment. It is believed that constant attention to the mind may gear up the learning process. Educating the mind is a process whereby all activities are concentrated on the purpose of achieving positive results. All learners may have to yield to proliferation of the audacity to learn new ideas to attain success.

Education is an absolutely necessity to survive the efficacies of the well being of individuals in the society. Through education, there can be pathways for political, social, and economic stability in the society.

The objectivity of the institutions and the communities alike depends on the social norms of educational facilities and institutions. Education as portrayed by society can be engaged in all sorts of forms. It is certain that response to changes is dominantly recognized. Both society and individual educators and learners must be aware of the fact that the spontaneous adaptabilities and objectivities of the characteristics of consciousness rest on the longevity of humans. As human beings evolved through life, the ability to learn new ideas and assimilate the ideas increases. According to the great philosopher, Darwin, "The most dominant and successful persons are the most response to changes". Learners turned to education in response to changes in their life.

The perseverance of institutions and their objects or facilities depends on the society conceptions and perceptions of education and its contents. What is it that is to be learned and thought in these institutions? The tasks must be obliterated in some form or ways. The incumbents as learners must recognize the security and motivational needs of the communities and the society as whole.

There is a controversial view as to who are really the educators in our society. Since there is always a change in the adaptability and objectivity of all individuals, educators could really be anyone who is capable of the intensity to changes. Some learners have control over what they want to learn, the educators do not have control over what is to be thought and taught, and therefore it is lifelong learning experience for both the learners and educators.

The bond between learners and educators is a sophistication prerogative of who is really learning and educating. It is assumed that both the learners and educators learned from each other. The experiences of everyone depend on the substance of needs of the society and individual. The well-being of people in the society depends on the orientation approach to the needs and security of individual. Communities and society often actively seek education quality to the fullest, so as to enlighten the individuals in society and reap the outcomes. In this process, leadership prospects emerge.

It should not be forgotten that to be successful, one must compromise. The leaders and those that are being led must contribute their individual quotas to the decision makings, same goes for learners and educators. This is to say that there must be probing actions of everyone involved.

Leading is a template of success. Every connotation of actions MUST BE analyzed to the best ability of the leader.

Purpose of Education

Education is through motivation and satisfying the needs of humans. The scientific world is part of an elongated human development. This can be substantiated with the use and evolution of TECHNOLGY. Educations of the entities that comprise the need to achieve the goal of TECHNOLOGY are important issues of today. Education is a conglomerate of beliefs in the individual mind.

The TECHNOLOGY world plays a role in this development. It can be said that TECHNOLOGY is based on strategic planning. It has been noted throughout history that ideas and inventions can be obtained through exploration and scientific abomination. Education is the foundation of continuity, sustainability, and transformation. The group of individual learners can be the sole of success of education.

We can achieve our needs through critical innovation of the mind regardless of our role in society. Everyone is a learner since we do not have control over what is to be learned. The circumstances surrounding education and its mode of delivery may be due to affordability and security. These in turn affect the volatility and the flexibility of learning.

To eliminate doubts and worry, education needs to justify the prosperity of societal factors. The incumbents involved must have the resources to attain their goals. Since we have various goals and needs, society or organization must always embed or include scenario and standard of accomplishments with their expectations.

The modalities of learning comprised all entities of understanding processes of humans. The dexterity of the mind can be explained through all means of communication. Both internal and external modes of communication can be justified in the development of intelligence.

The learning processes not only consist of spiritual processes, but all physical environmental and technological scientific means. The learning modes change as one progresses through the channel of dwelling of living. Society must realize that learning yield success only if it is applied substantially through the minds of the individuals. Individuals learned most under the assumptions that they possess already all the preliminary processes of life within society. As mentioned in one of the seminar sessions in Tucson, Arizona, in the United States of America, we as humans tend to have assumptions that we can do everything. Acquiring self-knowledge always demands self-reflection. There is absolutely no way we can get to know ourselves if we don't take some quiet time to meditate. Contemplation is another one of the ways WE tend to learn. We are willing mostly to open to ideas and will try untested approaches and accept risk of learning. When people are at their personal best, their projects or activities involve creative thinking and beyond-the-boundary thinking because of the atmospheric conditions accorded to them during the process of learning.

Even though we have gone through a process at an early stage, we must realize that.

Nothing is done perfectly the very first time, not in schools, not in sports, not in games and certainly not in communities. We must also understand that as humans evolve through changes that humans tend to search for learning opportunities. Opportunities that will meet the current changes and the foresee changes. The future changes may depend on the learning materials of the present.

Changes may involve physical, psychological, and social changes as opposed to environmental changes in our society and schools. Education rests in the hands of the beholder. Education and science TECHNOLOGY are intrigues in our mind as important aspects of life as we progress through life. Education and science TECHNOLOGY are based on needs and consequences derived from the past. We all make mistakes; we must learn from our mistakes which is a form of making progress.

Education and Science TECHNOLOGY are based on the homogeity of physical resources available to us as humans. Our adaptation is the objectivity of our consciousness. It should be noted that contemptuous circumstances can be resolved through education.

Educating the mind IN ENSSENCE is prolific; we should engage in the learning process. Education is a process whereby we should all learn together regardless of who you are.

Community, identity, stability are the main characteristics of the methodology of education in society. As it is often conveyed in parabolic ways, stability is required of any individual, if he or she is to succeed in the society. And, in order for an individual to portray a positive identity within the society educational stability will have to play a vital ROLE IN acquiring knowledge. AS it is often said, Knowledge comes from learning and experience while learning and experience are respectively derived from trying and doing. Without stability and knowledge, it may be impossible to acquire success. Individuals may quest for knowledge, stability and success at early stage of their educational career, but these entities may later be suppressed at a later stage of their life.

The possibility of attaining all the individual goals may rest solely on the individual and the society at large.

The learning process depends on the motivational level of the individual which may encompass the ingredients of success. The ingredient of success in the society may determine the notions of knowledge and experience. Education as an art to prowess is the basis of integrity in the society as whole. The power of success is achievable through knowledge. The initial educational attributes of an individual suffice as learning takes place. Knowledge based ON experience at an initial stage may result in learning activity of the present.

Learning enterprise is a mode of which individual survived in the society. Accumulation of wealth may have to depend on the knowledge and experience in society, learning and success inevitably juxtaposed the amenities of wealth. The essence of educational training is the preparedness of the individual to stability and success. It must be addressed to the problematic situations of individuals in society.

The circumstances surrounding propagation of learning is not solely materialism, but on the gratitude of knowledge. The standard which knowledge and materialism is attained is repertoire of educational establishments. In rationalizing the commonwealth of training individual, the society should apply transformation and sustainability in the evolution of education and science. The extenuation of objectives depends on current and past activities.

The educational solitudes may result in self-actualization of goals and thereby create self-awareness.

The technicality of learning may be justified by the scope of activities in society. The education of the literate is different from that of illiterates in society. Literacy does not mean everything is known, there are lessons to be learned from everyday activities in the society. Illiteracy of the mind is tolerable in certain aspects of learning.

The integration of learning may depend on the theme that individual need to know the anthology of survival. Stability projects the purpose of learning new ideas in our world. The determination of success rests on stability and knowledge.

Education of the mind is congenial to the cognitive approach of learning environment. It is believed that constant attention to the mind may gear up the learning process. Educating the mind is a process whereby all activities are concentrated on the purpose of achieving POSITIVE results. Everyone must yield to proliferation of the audacity to learn new ideas to attain success in society.

CHAPTER VIII

Positiveness Attitudes

In ORDER TO ATTAIN SUCCESS IN ALL ENDEAVORS WE MUST HAVE POSITIVE ATTITUDES IN ALL OUR UNDERTAKINGS. TO ACHIEVE THE HIGH PERFORMANCE OF THE FACTORS OF THE ECONOMY IN TUMULTUOUS ENVIRONMENT, CONSIDERABLE AWARENESS SHOULD BE PLACED ON BETTER EDUCATION. Education of the citizens plays an enormous role in justifying the economic success of individuals and the overall society.

Education is the pillar of all good things. Without education we would go nowhere in accomplishing our ultimate goals. As was mentioned earlier in this book and in all my writings, we all learn every day; be it from our mistakes or from one another, which are forms of education. We should possess an attitude that education is for everyone; that education is a life- long learning process and that it can take place anywhere within our society of ours. It should be noted that we all learn from each other; In terms of the amount of prior knowledge and experience that one has, the difference between those who know a great deal about what they are experiencing and those who know very little is very important. A person can be an expert in a variety of areas from growing peanuts to flying aircraft or skiing. According to Sternberg, in one of his books; "Perhaps the most fundamental difference between those who know much (experts) and those who know little (novices) is that experts bring more knowledge to solving problem, and they do so more effectively than novices." Additionally, the so-called experts can able to solve problems faster and in more economical way. To be experts in removing the obstacles of tumultuous situations to achieve success, we must involve experts or those who know much about a situation, those who have self-monitoring skills, and those who are able to view and solve problems at deeper and immense levels than novices or those who know little.

To realize success, we must heed to the belief that nothing is impossible to accomplish. There is no end to educating the mind. Nearly all our activities involved some kind of training of the mind that is educational. Our attitudes toward learning or engagement in positive activities determine the success of individuals in tumultuous environments or situations. The behavioral approach to learning and the awareness of the necessary rudiments to be successful in turbulent situations must be implemented in all organizations, including educational settings.

PERFORMANCE ENHANCEMENT

IN ORDER TO EMBELLISH OR ENHANCE PERFORMANCE OF INDIVIDUAL IN THE SOCIETY, ALL AMENTIES OF EDUCATIONAL PROPRIETRY MUST BE TAKEN INTO CONSIDERATIONS. BOTH TECHNOLOGICAL ENTITIES: SOCIAL AND ECONOMIC AND ALIGNED CONDITIONS MUST BE THOROUGHLY EXPLORED ACCORDINGLY. The performance of an individual depends on how the economic and education infrastructures are managed. An individual's performance can be enhanced by utilizing all the resources available.

The optimum improvement of our knowledge would lead to enhancement of performance through education or training of our mind – formally or informally. Performance enhancement can be obtained or realized in any establishment and by individual people with positive utilization of knowledge through training and education. The educational resources are what improve the economy and social well-being of the society. We should not forget that the social conditions of individuals depend on both the economic and education resources available to them. Without proper education and stabilize economic climate, social climate and political climate, society would be or remain un-inhabited or unlivable.

Education or training serves as an enhancement to high performance of every individual in the society. Education or training provides coverage to what life has to offer. It would be an individual's prerogative to enhance their performances and protect themselves from obstacles in society. It should be noted that society dwells on the path of creations and education in order to embellish the utilization of resources available in the society. Everyone must learn to improve performance to better we or to make life easier for everyone. The obstacles or difficulties encountered in our daily life can be avoided if everyone learns the rhetoric of basic education and high-performance enhancements. Education always opens the door or provides an avenue of success to anyone who seeks success in his or her endeavors. Higher performance can be realized in education if the economic conditions attached to training or education are solvent in capital. Education is for wellbeing of individual as well for the betterment of society, both socially, economically, and politically. Enhancement of education would have to demand high performance improvement in all areas of society or individual involvements or in all activities.

AVAILABILITY OF RESOURCES

The availability of educational resources is an important aspect of achieving success in a turbulent environment. Education resources must be adequately made available to everyone in society to realize the ultimate use of knowledge. Technology as well as economical resources if used positively will solve many problems of tumultuous conditions of the society.

The stipends allotted to education would yield or solve the burdens encountered on the way to achieving success in the tumultuous environment if properly utilized. Stipends are not the only means of reaching a successful goal; all other resources would also have to be put to use positively. Educators and learners in all facets of establishments, both educational and non-educational environments must have the compromise to learn from each other and understand the rhetoric of education if success is to be realized in a turbulent condition, one must put his or her knowledge, and ability to optimum use. Past experiences will also exemplify the present process of eliminating the obstacles to success. One must always dwell or rely on positive facts and experiences. In a negative environment or negative condition, it may be necessary to adjust or adapt to all the conditions on the journey to success or "the promised land," so to speak.

The indulgence of politics or government in managing and regulating the activities of educational institutions should be minimized to an extent. This is not to say that Government should not be involved in the regulations of educational institutions. A large part of the involments should be left for individual institutions or organizations to be implemented, if we are to achieve success in all our endeavors. The control of resources must be shifted to individuals without political interference. Political regulations of institutions or organizations would interfere with their prosperity if it were not diligently managed and minimized with strong uphold.

There should be great support for institutions in terms of capital. Management in every institution should be able to implement all terms of objectives. Management should tremendously be able to use and stabilize the resources provided by the political system. The support from the political system must be taken advantage of by every educational and non-educational institution. The support provided by the political systems in the form of capital and other resources should be used solely for the benefits of the institutions.

EDUCATION RELATIONS

The issue of embracing relationships with external companies or institutions both locally and globally for the provisions of economic success is an important issue in a tumultuous environment. The lack of relationship with external establishments creates unjustifiable prospects for people in society. Non partnership with external congruence is very antagonizing. Relations with external companies or institutions would surely bring enormous prospects to individuals and society; and it would also encourage friendly companies or institutions to offer helping hands. The recruitment of graduates from the university's campus by companies has declined tremendously in recent years.

In the world of higher education, not only are academics of the students very important, the economics, sociology and ethics associated with well beings of individuals and the educators must be taken into consideration. To ensure a very positive economical, sociological, and ethical solution, there must be great deal of relationship or partnership with the external congruence within the society.

The external companies serve a purpose in the existence of educational establishments. Without external companies or organizations there would be nothing to look forward to in tumultuous environment or condition. By establishing partnerships with companies, individuals will be able have many options for prosperity.

It has been a tradition that companies ameliorate with others to increase their exposure, but there has been a decline of affiliations in recent years. To avoid chaos in a turbulent environment and to prosper economically and ethically educational relationship of individual and corporations must be a priority. Leaders, as well as the public must be able establish rapports with one another in the society.

Companies are now looking to academic institutions to provide research and development of products, including professional graduates, and services for the growing economy. The tests for educational institutions and organizations are the balancing of the social demands with the academic and economic problems already established.

The situation of people having no experience brings about the importance of networking to secure proper avenues of success. It is very important that we create relationships with outsiders, since this will be beneficial, especially to the whole society. With the society in tumultuous conditions, there will be a massive incapable supply of general education professionals. Therefore, a plan of employment as to where individual professionals will fit in in the society is needed. The creation of partnerships with outside companies, organizations and education institutions within society would enable professionals to secure jobs, and institutions to obtain grants, and good public relations from the companies and organizations.

If we concentrate on the establishment of relationships with the external congruence, then we would be able to achieve success in all our endeavors and would create a good image for ourselves and the society at large; growth and evolution of innovations may also well be explosive. For example, if we engage in more relationships with private local and external industries to enable employment, research, program development and dissemination of knowledge, then our economic, social and ethics will surpass average.

The benefits derived from being partners with outsiders may surpass conditions of not. Being a partner with institutional establishments does not necessarily guarantee economic success, neither does it guarantee the realization of our goal, but it is "a steppingstone" to success or a foot at the door to success. If we establish friendship with external congruence, an advantage may be given to individual when it comes to doing favors or engaging in research, innovations, and program development to disseminating knowledge. If we do not concentrate on creating partnership with outsiders, we may find ourselves in bad situations or remain in tumultuous conditions whereby we would only have few resources for development, and we may not be globally recognized. We may have to fiercely compete for resources in the global market. We should all come to terms those nurturing relationships in education or partnership is important.

EPITOME
This book is dedicated
To my late brother:

LT. Col. Akinyele Francis Kejawa Of Nigeria

One can
PROLONG LIFE
Or extend Life
BECAUSE INFINITY
IS
The WAY
OF
L I F E † Because infinity is the Way of life

****

ADAGES OF OUR TIME

"So Shall It Be" "Great Minds Discuss Ideas; Average Minds
Discuss Events While Minds Discuss People."
Eleneanor Roosevelt.

"Put Your Head Under the Umbrella so Thou Shall not be
Troubled."
Dr. Iwasan D. Kejawa

"The Logeivity of Human is the Homogeneity of their Body and the Spontaneity
of their Adaptability is the Objectivity of their Consciousness."
Dr. Iwasan D. Kejawa

"Educations is our passport to the future for tomorrow belongs
to the those who prepares for it today." MALCOM X.

"Education is not an end, but a means to an end." MARTIN LUGHTER KING.

It is not Only What Do but What you Know and How you
Apply What you Know to your Life Endeavors."
DR. IWASAN D. KEJAWA

"LIFE IS THAT OF A BIRD IN THE AIR, LIFE TAKES
YOU
EVERYWHERE."

THE AUTHOR

Prof. Dr. Iwasan D. Kejawa was born at Erekiti village in Ondo State west part of Nigeria, west Africa. He migrated to Lagos, Nigeria in the seventies. He then went to complete his secondary school studies at Republic of Benin (then known as Dahomey). He worked briefly as International Telephone Operator at Nigerian External Telecommunications in Lagos.

Dr. Kejawa Migrated to the United States of America in the eighties and Studied at City University of New York, earning a bachelor's and master's Degrees. He later relocated to Florida to further his education at Nova Southeastern University, earning a Doctorate in education.

Dr. Kejawa is an educator and writer by profession; He has published various articles in reputable international journals or magazines. He has also published several books on education, technology, mathematics, business, computer science and other literature.

Dr. Iwasan D. Kejawa is currently a Professor at Miami Dade College and Palm Beach State College in the United States.